W9-AOV-517

A

A New True Book

ANIMAL OBSERVATIONS

By Ray Broekel

CHILDRENS PRESS®

CHICAGO

Can you guess what this is? It is the tadpole of an American toad.

For Pola, Fergus, and BB—all lefties

Library of Congress Cataloging-in-Publication Data

Broekel, Ray.
   Animal observations / by Ray Broekel.
      p.   cm. — (A New true book)
   Includes index.
   Summary: Discusses the behavior and the habitats
of different kinds of animals and what can be learned
by observing birds, mammals, insects, and other kinds
of wildlife.
   ISBN 0-516-01182-0
   1. Animals—Juvenile literature.   2.   Wildlife
watching—Juvenile literature.   [1.   Animals.
2.   Wildlife watching.]   I.   Title.
QL49.B746   1990   89-25363
591—dc20   CIP
                                            AC

PHOTO CREDITS
© Reinhard Brucker—7, 37 (top & bottom right)

© Cameramann International Ltd.—6 (right), 8
(bottom left)

© Alan & Sandy Carey—43 (right)

© Jerry Hennen—8 (top left), 13 (right & bottom
left), 19 (center right), 24 (left), 28 (left), 29, 33
(top & bottom right)

© Norma Morrison—11 (right)

Photri—19 (top left); © Photri/Lani, 10 (left)

R/C Photo Agency—© Richard L. Capps, 12 (right),
13 (top left), 37 (left), 39 (right)

Root Resources—© Gail Nachel, 41 (left); © Mary
A. Root, 45 (bottom left)

Tom Stack & Associates—© David M. Dennis, 2;
© Mary Clay, 14 (left); © Robert C. Simpson, 19 (top
right); © Leonard Lee Rue III, 21 (right & top left);
© Don and Esther Phillips, 23 (left); © John
Cancalosi, 24 (right); © John Shaw, 28 (center &
right); © John Gerlach, 34, 35; © Jack Swenson, 44
(right); © Brian Parker, 44 (left)

Lynn Stone—4 (top right), 8 (right & center), 27
(right), 33 (left), 39 (left), 40, 41 (right), 42 (2
photos)

Valan—© Thomas Kitchin, Cover, 4 (center left), 17
(right); © Halle Flygare, 4 (bottom left); © Herman
Giethoorn, 4 (bottom right), 45 (top right); © Gilbert
van Ryckevorsel, 4 (top left); © V. Wilkinson, 6
(left); © J. Eastcott/Y. Momatiuk, 9; © Irwin Barrett,
10 (right); © Harold V. Green, 11 (left), 24 (center);
© Murray O'Neill, 12 (left); © S. J. Krasemann, 12
(center); © Pam Hickman, 14 (right); © M. Julien, 15
(right); © R. C. Simpson, 15 (left); © Jeff Foott, 16,
43 (left); © Tom W. Parkin, 17 (left); © Mrs. Mildred
McPhee, 19 (bottom right); © Wayne Lankinen, 21
(bottom left), 45 (top left); © Michel Bourque, 23
(right); © John Fowler, 27 (left); © J. A. Wilkinson,
31 (left); © Val & Alan Wilkinson, 31 (right);
© Richard T. Nowitz, 45 (bottom right)

Cover: Wildlife in the City

TABLE OF CONTENTS

The tiger (above) and the wolf (bottom left) are meat eaters (carnivores). The moose (left) and parakeets (below) are plant eaters (herbivores). The snapping turtle (top left) eats plants and meat. It is called an omnivore.

WHAT IS AN ANIMAL?

An animal is a living thing that is not a plant. Most animals can move and feel, but they cannot make their own food.

Some animals eat plants. Plant eaters are called herbivores. Some animals eat other animals. Meat eaters are called carnivores.

Some animals eat both plant and animal foods. They are called omnivores.

WILDLIFE AND DOMESTIC ANIMALS

Animals that live in the wild are called wildlife. These animals take care of themselves.

Some animals help people. Long ago, people tamed these animals. They are raised for food, or for

Chickens (left) and dairy cows (right) are domestic animals.

Horses pulled
plows before
tractors were
invented.

work, or for other things.
These animals are called
domestic animals. They
need people to feed and
care for them.

Cattle are raised for meat
and milk. Chickens are
raised for meat and eggs.
Horses are raised to do work.

Rabbits (top left), birds (bottom left), dogs (center), and cats (right) are popular pets.

What kinds of domestic animals are found where you live?

Many people keep animals as pets. What kinds of pets are found in your neighborhood? Observe them.

RIGHT-PAWED OR LEFT-PAWED?

Is your dog right-pawed or left-pawed? Try this simple experiment.

Play ball with your dog. Notice which paw the dog uses the most. Think of other ways to observe which paw

Which paw is this dog using to "shake hands"?

the dog uses most. Which paw does the dog use to scratch on the door when it wants to come in? Is the dog a lefty or a righty?

What about your cat? Is your cat left-pawed or right-pawed? Be sure to make a number of observations before making your decision.

EXPLORE YOUR NEIGHBORHOOD

Do you live in the country
or in the city? Do you live
where there are lots of trees
or where there are no trees?

What kinds of wild animals
are found where you live?

Look for wildlife in the air
and on the ground.

Wildlife can be found in the country or in the city.

Deer (left) live in woodlands, bighorn sheep (center) live in mountains, and loons (right) live near water.

DIFFERENT HABITATS

Different animals live in different kinds of places. These places are called habitats. A place with lots of trees is called a woodland habitat. Certain kinds of wildlife live in a woodland habitat.

The kit fox (bottom left) and the cactus wren (above) live in deserts. The river otter (top left) lives near water.

In a desert habitat, you will see different kinds of wildlife. There are other kinds of habitats, too. What kinds of wildlife live in lakes, oceans, rivers, or ponds? Do the same kinds of wildlife live in fresh water as in salt water?

OBSERVING WILDLIFE – FOOD

What do the different kinds of wildlife in your neighborhood eat? Robins are wildlife. Observe what these birds eat. Are robins herbivores, carnivores, or omnivores?

A robin (left) has caught a worm. A flower crab spider (right) kills a bee. Both are carnivores.

Many kinds of spiders catch their food in webs (left). The painted turtle (right), like most turtles, is an omnivore.

What about different kinds of spiders? What do spiders catch in their webs? Are spiders carnivores?

What about other wildlife? Make a list with the following headings: Herbivores, Carnivores, and Omnivores. List the animals you observe under the proper heading.

OBSERVING WILDLIFE – BIRDS

How many toes does a bird have? It depends on the kind of bird.

The roadrunner lives in a desert habitat. It uses its four toes to help it run. Two toes point forward, and two toes point backward.

Roadrunner

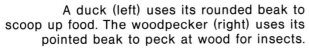
A duck (left) uses its rounded beak to scoop up food. The woodpecker (right) uses its pointed beak to peck at wood for insects.

Woodpeckers use their toes to help them climb trees. Ducks use their webbed feet to swim.

We can observe birds and other wildlife in our own area. But what about wildlife in other habitats? How can we find out about them?

17

Look them up in bird books. We can find out things about wild animals by reading about them as well as by observing them.

What kinds of nests do birds build? That depends on the kind of bird. The Baltimore oriole builds a hanging nest.

The male Baltimore oriole is more colorful than the female. Orioles eat insects that are caught near the tops of trees.

Baltimore orioles (above) build a nest of vegetable fibers. Cardinals (center) weave nests of twigs and grass. Barn swallows (bottom) build nests of mud.

Look for other bird nests. Note what kinds of birds nest in them. Make a list of the kinds of birds you watch.

OBSERVING WILDLIFE – MAMMALS

Be careful when observing wild animals. Watch them from a distance. Never try to handle a wild animal.

Raccoons are found in wooded areas and like to live near water. But they are also found where people live.

Raccoons eat such things as insects, mice, crabs, fish, and vegetables. Raccoons that live near people may sometimes eat garbage.

Raccoons like to raid garbage cans and bring food back to their tree den. Observe the face markings.

In the wild, raccoons build their dens in a hollow tree or in a cave. In the city, they may build their dens in chimneys. Raccoons usually look for

21

food at night. You can observe them at night, or very early in the morning.

Squirrels live where there are trees. The gray squirrel eats foods from plants, such as nuts.

Observe the way squirrels get about. Do they run up and down trees? How do they act when they run on the ground? Watch young squirrels at play.

Baby squirrels are born in nests in tree hollows or in

Squirrels build their nests with twigs and leaves.

nests built high in trees. Look
for squirrel nests in the winter
when the trees are bare.

Chipmunks eat nuts, fruits,
and the seeds of trees such as
maple, oak, and elm.

Chipmunks can climb
trees. They are comfortable

Chipmunks (left and center) are fun to watch.
The opossum (right) likes to hang upside down in trees.

around people. They
sometimes make their nests
in garages or in stone walls.

Observe how a chipmunk
holds its tail while running. Is
it straight up or is it out flat?

The opossum lives in

wooded areas, but it can be found in cities. Like the raccoon, the opossum looks for food at night.

The opossum eats almost anything. It likes eggs, persimmons, and insects.

An opossum is about the size of a house cat. It climbs trees using its feet and tail. Observe an opossum moving about. Does it move fast or slow?

What other kinds of mammals can you observe where you live?

OBSERVING WILDLIFE – INSECTS

Insects are the most common kinds of animal life in the world. You can observe them easily.

Observe an anthill. How do the ants build it? Where do the ants go when they leave the nest? Do they bring anything back?

The monarch butterfly is an insect that lays its eggs on milkweed plants.

A monarch butterfly egg (left), shown here
many times life size. Monarch caterpillars (right)

Find some milkweed
plants. Then look for the
eggs on the undersides of
the leaves. Watch the eggs
to see the caterpillars hatch.

The caterpillars eat the
plants after hatching. They
grow quickly because they
eat all the time.

The monarch chrysalis (left and center) gradually darkens.
Then the adult butterfly comes out (right).

Observe the caterpillar
when it goes into the
chrysalis stage. Inside this
shell, the caterpillar changes
into an adult monarch
butterfly.

The butterfly comes out
of the chrysalis in the
summer. In the fall, it flies

south to a warmer place.

Observe the monarchs as they fly. Do they fly in straight lines? Or do they seem to jump about as they fly?

The praying mantis is the only insect that can look over its own shoulder. The mantis eats insects such as flies and grasshoppers.

The mantis is not harmful to people, but the female mantis often eats the male after laying her eggs.

Observe how a mantis moves about. How does it use its front pair of legs?

The ladybug, or ladybird, is a kind of beetle. Ladybugs are very helpful to people because both the adult and the caterpillar or larvae eat aphids. Aphids are insects that are harmful to plants.

There are many kinds of ladybugs. What kinds are found where you live?

You can identify different kinds of ladybugs by the number and color of spots

The ladybug (left) eats aphids. Right: Fireflies (right) give off their own light, which blinks off and on.

on their backs. One kind has two spots. Another kind has nine spots.

Observe ladybugs feeding. See how many kinds of ladybugs you can find.

What other kinds of insects can you observe where you live?

OBSERVING WILDLIFE – REPTILES AND AMPHIBIANS

Reptiles are cold-blooded animals. Snakes, lizards, and turtles are reptiles.

Amphibians are cold-blooded animals that live part of their lives in water and part of their lives on land. Frogs, salamanders, and toads are amphibians. You can observe the tadpoles of frogs and toads in water.

Snakes (left) and
alligators (top right)
are reptiles. Toads
(bottom right) are
amphibians.

You can observe many adult
frogs and toads on land.

What other kinds of
reptiles can you observe
where you live?

Lizards are often found in
dry or desert habitats. The

Fence lizard

fence lizard lives around
fallen woody plants. It also
likes places that are
somewhat dry. It does not
harm people and eats many
insects. The fence lizard
likes sunlight.

Observe how a fence

lizard catches its food. Are

Yosemite
toad

its toes short and stubby, or long and slender?

Toads are amphibians. As adults they are often found in fields or gardens. Toads eat many kinds of insects and other small animal life.

Observe a toad as it looks for food. What does it do with its tongue?

OBSERVING WILDLIFE – FISH

There are over 20,000 kinds of fish. Some live in fresh water. Others live in salt water.

Fish breathe by means of gills. Oxygen is removed from the water as it passes through the gills.

You can observe fish in a small aquarium.

Observe where the fish swim. Do they swim at the

The Siamese fighting
fish (top right) and the
neon tetra (bottom right)
are popular aquarium
fish (top left).

top or in the middle or at the
bottom? Where do the young
fish swim? Where do the
adult fish swim?

Where do the fish feed
when food is dropped into
the water?

OBSERVING ZOO ANIMALS

Animals that live in your part of the world are called native animals.

Animals that are not native to your area can be seen in zoos or in aquariums.

Visit a zoo and observe how a kangaroo uses its legs and tail.

Giraffes (left) and kangaroos (right) can be observed in zoos.

See how the giraffe's long neck helps it to feed on leaves high up in trees.

When the giraffe wants to reach something on the ground, how does it bend its legs? Observe how it uses its legs when running.

Observe other zoo
animals. How do they move
about? Do they use body
parts other than their legs to
move about? How does the
elephant use its trunk?

In spring, piglets are born and bloodroot flowers bloom.

THE SEASONS

Observe the signs of
spring around you. What is
happening?

In spring, many animals
give birth to their young—and
plants start to grow again.

Those plants will be food
for many of the animals.

41

Above: Mother sheep and lamb
Baby ducklings (left) stay
close to their mothers.

Summer is the season
when most animals born in
spring grow up. There is
plenty to eat and the parents
have the summer months to
raise their young. The young
will be ready to go out on
their own in the fall.

Elk tracks in the snow (right) and Canada geese (left) flying south

In fall, some animals
migrate to a warmer place.
And in winter, some animals
hibernate—they fall into a
kind of sleep that protects
them from cold and hunger.
Look for animal tracks in
the snow or on wet ground.

43

FUTURE PLANS

Snails (left) and earthworms (right) are found in lawns and gardens.

What else can you observe about animal life? Make a list of things you can do in the future.

Watch small animals such as snails and earthworms. How does a snail move about? Observe the weather when earthworms are seen. Is it a nice day or a rainy day? Why do you see earthworms on days like that?

White-throated sparrow (top left), an ant colony (top right),
polar bears in a zoo (bottom left), and a city pigeon (bottom right)

Keep an animal notebook.
Make notes on what you
observe. Learn all you can
about the animal life around
you. And have fun doing it!

45

WORDS YOU SHOULD KNOW

amphibian(am • FIB • ee • yun) — a class of cold-blooded animals adapted for life both on land and in water

bird(BERD) — a warm-blooded, feathered animal with two feet and wings

carnivore(KAR • nih • vore) — meat eater

chrysalis(KRISS • uh • liss) — the form of the butterfly between the caterpillar and the adult stage

domestic animal(doh • MESS • tik   AN • ih • mil) — an animal that is tame and raised for food or work, or kept as a pet

gills(GIHLZ) — the breathing organs of fish and other animals that live underwater

habitat(HAB • ih • tat) — the place where a plant or animal normally grows or lives

herbivore(HER • bih • vore) — plant eater

hibernate(HYE • ber • nate) — to spend the winter sleeping or dormant, as bears do

identify(i • DEN • tih • fye) — to prove something to be a certain kind of thing

insect(IN • sekt) — any of a large class of animals with three body segments, six legs, and usually two pairs of wings

larva(LAR • vah) — the caterpillar stage of an insect, after it hatches from the egg

mammal(MAM • il) — an animal with a backbone; female mammals produce milk for their young

native(NAY • tihv) — living naturally in a particular area or place

observe(ob • ZERV) — to see or notice; to watch attentively; to make careful examination of

omnivore(AHM • nih • vore) — animal that eats both plants and meat

oxygen(OX • ih • jin) — a colorless, odorless, tasteless gas that animals cannot live without

pet(PEHT) — a tame animal kept by a human

reptile(REHP • tyle) — any of a class of cold-blooded animals that crawl on their bellies or creep on very short legs

wildlife(WYLDE • lyfe) — animals or plants in the natural or wild state

INDEX

About the Author

Ray Broekel is well known as a teacher, editor, and author of books for young people. Over the years, Dr. Broekel has carried out many observations of animals. Two of his favorite animals were Sammy the Shrew and Henry the Hog-nosed Snake.

Dr. Broekel has written over 200 books. His first book was published by Childrens Press in 1956. He now lives with his wife Peg and their dog BB in Ipswich, Massachusetts.